MODERN SELLING TECHNIQUES:

Revolutionizing Your Sales Strategy for Today's Market

Fidel L. Jones

TABLE OF CONTENT

CHAPTER ONE

Introduction

Modern selling methods relate to the strategies and tactics employed by sales professionals to engage and convince prospective consumers successfully. These strategies have changed to match clients' changing demands and tastes in today's digital world.

Some current selling strategies include:

1. **Social Selling:** Using social media platforms like LinkedIn, Twitter, and Facebook to engage with prospective consumers and create connections.

2. **Personalization:** Tailoring sales communications to fit consumers' unique wants and preferences.

3. **Data-driven Selling:** Using data analytics to uncover patterns and trends in consumer behavior and preferences, enabling sales professionals to better anticipate and react to customer demands.

4. **Value Selling:** Focusing on the product or service's value to the consumer rather than just selling features and perks.

5. **Solution Selling:** Identifying the customer's pain spots and giving a personalized solution to those difficulties.

6. **Consultative Selling:** Acting as a consultant to the client, giving advice

and direction throughout the sales process.

7. **Storytelling:** Using tales and anecdotes to explain how the product or service has benefitted other consumers, generating a feeling of trust and trustworthiness.

8. **Multi-channel Selling:** Utilizing several channels, such as email, phone, and social media, to contact prospective clients and deliver a smooth purchase experience.

9. **Relationship Selling:** Focusing on creating long-term connections with consumers rather than completing a one-time transaction.

Overall, contemporary selling strategies emphasize creating connections with consumers, giving value, and responding to the changing demands and preferences of the modern buyer.

Background of selling

Selling has been around for thousands of years and has played a crucial part in business and trade. Throughout history, selling has developed and adapted to new technology, market situations, and client preferences.

In ancient times, selling was commonly performed in open-air marketplaces or bazaars, where sellers would showcase their wares and bargain with possible consumers. As civilizations got more sophisticated and urbanized, selling became more specialized, with merchants specializing in certain items and services, such as textiles, spices, or precious metals.

With the rise of industrialization in the 18th and 19th centuries, selling became more institutionalized, with corporations utilizing sales staff to advertise their goods and services to clients. The emergence of mass media, such as newspapers and radio, in the 20th century allowed firms new opportunities to contact people and market their goods.

In the late 20th century, the development of the internet and e-commerce transformed selling once again, with corporations embracing online methods to contact clients and sell their goods. Today, selling is more data-driven and customer-centric than ever before, with sales professionals employing sophisticated analytics and digital technologies to tailor their approach and give value to clients.

Throughout history, selling has been a vital business component, helping enterprises contact clients, advertise their goods and services, and drive economic progress.

The Evolution of Selling

Selling has experienced tremendous development, reflecting sociological, technical, and economic changes. The following are some of the main phases in the development of selling:

The Barter System:

The barter system is regarded as one of the first types of commercial trade and is a forerunner to contemporary selling. While it may not be seen as a progression of selling in the usual sense, it did include exchanging products and services, a basic selling component.

In the barter system, individuals swap one thing or service for another without using cash. This system was prevalent in ancient periods and continued to be utilized in many regions of the globe until the emergence of modern monetary systems.

Bartering entailed the exchange of commodities or services of equal value, and talks would take place between the persons involved to define the conditions of the trade. Bartering enabled individuals to get the things or services they needed without utilizing money, which was yet to be a standardized means of exchange.

While the barter system is not directly connected to current selling, it did entail the exchange of commodities and services, which is a key principle in selling. The barter system also needed negotiating and communication skills, which are vital in current marketing. Additionally, the barter system underlines the significance of knowing the requirements and preferences of prospective clients, which is a vital component of contemporary selling.

Door-to-Door Sales:

Door-to-door sales is an evolution of selling since it significantly changed how things were advertised and sold to clients. Before the introduction of door-to-door sales in the 19th century, most purchases happened in retail establishments or via personal ties.

Door-to-door sales entailed sales associates traveling directly to the homes of prospective consumers to display and offer things. This strategy enabled salespeople to contact a greater number of clients in a more customized way since they could adjust their sales presentation to the requirements and tastes of each customer.

Door-to-door sales also forced salespeople to have good communication and persuasive abilities since they needed to persuade clients to make a purchase based on a brief conversation. Additionally, door-to-door sales required salespeople to be informed about their goods since they needed to address any questions or concerns that prospective consumers may have.

Door-to-door sales became especially popular in the mid-20th century with the expansion of suburbs and increased house ownership. While door-to-door sales have dropped in prominence in recent years owing to the advent of digital marketing and e-commerce, they remain an essential part of the sales landscape for some kinds of goods, such as home security systems and pest control services.

Overall, door-to-door sales may be considered an evolution of selling since it marked a substantial change in how items were advertised and sold, forcing salespeople to learn new skills and techniques to be successful.

Retail Stores:

Retail shops may be considered an important development in selling since they signified a move from door-to-door sales to a more centralized and accessible sales strategy. Retail shops enabled consumers to peruse a range of things in one area, and salespeople were stationed throughout the store to help customers with their purchases.

The rise of retail outlets in the late 19th and early 20th centuries enabled corporations to reach more clients more efficiently and cost-effectively. Retail establishments also offered a more stable and predictable environment for selling since salespeople could depend on a continuous stream of foot traffic and did not have to rely primarily on personal connections with consumers.

Retail establishments needed salespeople to gain new abilities, such as product knowledge, merchandising, and customer service, to be successful. Salespeople at retail establishments were generally responsible for replenishing shelves, arranging displays, and resolving client queries and concerns.

Retail shops also enabled corporations to participate in new types of advertising and promotion, such as in-store displays and signage, which might help attract consumers and improve sales.

Overall, retail outlets may be considered a key progression of selling, since they signified a move from individualized door-to-door sales to a more centralized and accessible sales strategy. Retail shops encouraged salespeople to learn new skills and techniques to be effective and enabled corporations to participate in new types of advertising and marketing to reach more consumers.

Telemarketing:

Telemarketing is a new option for firms to contact consumers via a direct connection over the phone. Telemarketing began in the mid-20th century and rapidly became a popular sales tactic for various goods and services.

Telemarketing enables salespeople to contact many prospective consumers quickly and effectively without face-to-face engagement. Telemarketers might contact prospective consumers, offer items or services, answer queries, and complete purchases over the phone.

Telemarketing forced salespeople to learn new abilities, such as phone etiquette, persuasive communication, and overcoming obstacles. Telemarketers generally worked from call centers, where they were watched and educated to enhance their sales success.

Telemarketing also enabled organizations to target certain demographics and client groups, utilizing data analytics and other methods to find prospective customers who were most likely to be interested in their goods or services.

While telemarketing has grown less popular in recent years owing to rising regulation and customer opposition, it remains an essential component of the sales landscape for specific kinds of goods and services. Many firms use telemarketing to contact new consumers and complete sales, especially in insurance, telecommunications, and financial services. Overall, telemarketing may be considered an evolution of selling since it provides a new means for corporations to contact clients via direct conversation over the phone, forcing salespeople to learn new skills and techniques to be effective.

Direct Mail:

Direct mail may be considered an evolution of selling since it introduced a new approach for corporations to engage clients via focused, individualized postal campaigns. Direct mail arose in the mid-20th century as a means for corporations to deliver promotional materials directly to prospective consumers' homes.

Direct mail campaigns enabled firms to contact many prospective consumers with a customized message that could be adjusted to their interests and requirements. Direct mail campaigns involve some items, including letters, pamphlets, flyers, and product samples.

Direct mail marketing encouraged salespeople to learn new talents, such as copywriting, graphic design, and data analytics. Salespeople were responsible for producing appealing content and resources that attract the attention of prospective consumers and generate sales.

Direct mail campaigns also enabled organizations to target certain demographics and client groups, utilizing data analytics and other technologies to find prospective customers who were most likely to be interested in their goods or services.

While direct mail campaigns have grown less popular in recent years due to rising digital marketing and e-commerce, they remain an essential component of the sales landscape for specific goods and services. Many organizations continue to employ direct mail campaigns to contact new consumers and boost sales, especially in banking, healthcare, and real estate.

Overall, direct mail may be considered an evolution of selling since it provides a new approach for corporations to engage clients via focused, individualized postal campaigns, forcing salespeople to learn new skills and techniques to be effective.

Digital Marketing:

Digital marketing is a fundamental selling progression since it signified a dramatic change in how organizations reach and connect with prospective consumers. Digital marketing includes leveraging digital channels such as search engines, social media, email, and websites to advertise goods and services and establish consumer connections.

Digital marketing provides several benefits over conventional techniques of selling. For example, it helps organizations reach a worldwide audience quickly and effectively and target certain demographics and client groups more accurately. Digital marketing also helps organizations manage and assess their efforts more effectively, using data analytics and other tools to monitor website traffic, social media participation, and other key performance indicators.

Digital marketing demands salespeople to adopt new skills and methods to be effective. Salespeople must know the newest digital marketing tools and practices, including search engine optimization (SEO), pay-per-click (PPC) advertising, social media marketing, email marketing, and content marketing.

Digital marketing also demands salespeople to be competent at developing interesting and appealing content that connects with their target audience. This may contain anything from blog articles and social media updates to films, infographics, and interactive tools.

Overall, digital marketing is a fundamental development of selling since it marks a substantial change in how organizations reach and connect with prospective clients. Digital marketing demands salespeople to learn new skills and methods to be effective, and it gives

Several benefits over conventional means of selling, including the capacity to reach a worldwide audience quickly and inexpensively, target certain demographics and client groups more precisely and monitor and assess the performance of campaigns more accurately.

Relationship Selling:

Relationship selling is an evolution of selling, as it signifies a change in emphasis from transactional selling to creating long-term, mutually beneficial relationships with clients. Relationship selling is a customer-centric strategy that stresses understanding and addressing the requirements of individual consumers rather than merely pushing items or services.

Relationship selling entails creating trust and relationships with consumers, listening to their wants and problems, and giving customized solutions that match their requirements. Relationship selling also requires continual contact and follow-up with clients to guarantee their happiness and find new prospects for sales and service.

Relationship selling encourages salespeople to learn new abilities, like active listening, empathy, and problem-solving. Salespeople must connect successfully with clients, create trust and rapport, and anticipate and handle customer requirements and problems.

Relationship selling also demands a change in thinking from a short-term, transactional emphasis to a long-term, relationship-building focus. Salespeople must be ready to devote time and effort to creating solid, mutually beneficial relationships with clients rather than merely making fast sales and moving on to the next prospect.

Relationship selling may be considered an evolution, as it indicates a change in emphasis from transactional selling to creating long-term, mutually beneficial connections with clients. Relationship selling requires salespeople to learn new skills and methods to be effective. It stresses the significance of knowing and addressing the requirements of individual clients to form strong, enduring connections.

Why Modern Selling Techniques Matter

Modern selling strategies are important because they enable sales professionals to adapt to today's clients' changing wants and tastes. With the growth of e-commerce, social media, and other digital platforms, consumers have more alternatives than ever when researching and buying goods and services. Consequently, sales professionals must be able to interact and influence clients across various channels and touchpoints successfully.

Modern selling approaches are also significant because they help sales professionals to develop better, more meaningful connections with consumers. Today's consumers seek more than simply goods and services - they want customized experiences, solutions, and real ties with their business organizations. By adopting current selling strategies, sales professionals may create these experiences and establish consumer trust and loyalty over time.

Finally, current selling strategies are important because they assist salespeople in keeping ahead of the competition. With so many firms fighting for the attention and money of clients, it's crucial to have a sales approach that stands out from the crowd. By employing current selling strategies, sales professionals may distinguish themselves and their firms and position themselves as trusted advisers and partners to their clients.

Overall, current selling strategies are important because they help sales professionals to adapt to changing client demands and preferences, create closer connections with customers, and remain ahead of the competition. By adopting current selling strategies, sales professionals may achieve better success and generate development for themselves and their organizations.

CHAPTER TWO

Understanding Your Customer

Understanding your consumer is vital for every organization that wants to prosper. It entails acquiring insights about your target audience, their requirements, tastes, and behavior. Knowing your consumers, you can personalize your goods, services, and marketing messages to match their requirements, which may help you develop great connections, produce more sales, and enhance customer loyalty.

Here are some crucial measures to take while seeking to understand your customers:

1. **Define your target audience:** Define them and know their demographics, psychographics, and behavior. This helps you personalize your marketing messaging and product offers to their demands.

2. **Conduct market research:** Market research may help you get insights into your consumers' requirements, tastes, and behavior. This may be done via surveys, focus groups, or by examining industry reports and data.

3. **Build customer personas:** Customer personas are imaginary characters that reflect your target demographic. By establishing customer personas, you may better know your consumers and personalize your marketing messages and product offers to their individual requirements.

4. **Engage with your consumers:** Engaging with your customers via social media, customer service, and other channels will assist you in understanding their wants and preferences. You may also utilize this feedback to enhance your goods and services.

5. **Use analytics:** Analyzing client data may help you understand their behavior, preferences, and requirements. You may use tools like Google Analytics to measure website traffic, engagement, and conversion rates.

Knowing your consumers, you can personalize your goods, services, and marketing messages to match their requirements, which may help you develop great connections, produce more sales, and enhance customer loyalty.

The Importance of Empathy in Sales

Empathy is a vital quality for sales associates to have. When salespeople can put themselves in their customer's shoes and understand their requirements, fears, and desires, they may form a relationship and build trust. This connection and trust are crucial to developing strong, long-lasting client connections.

Here are some reasons why empathy is vital in sales:

Understanding the customer's requirements

Understanding the customer's wants is a critical part of effective sales. When salespeople can understand the client's precise requirements and objectives, they may provide solutions that fulfill those demands and bring value to the consumer. Here are some recommendations on how to understand the customer's needs:

1. **Listen actively:**When communicating with consumers, listening to what they are saying is crucial. Please pay attention to their words, tone, and body language to better understand their wants and worries.

2. **Ask open-ended questions:** Open-ended inquiries allow consumers to disclose more information about their wants and aspirations. These inquiries also allow

salespeople to find wants the client may not have first expressed.

3. **explain their demands:** When clients communicate their wants, it's crucial to explain and validate their needs to ensure that salespeople properly understand them. This may ensure that salespeople can give the proper solutions.

4. **Observe their behavior:** How consumers engage with goods or services may give significant insights into their wants and preferences. Salespeople may utilize this information to modify their suggestions and give solutions matching the customer's demands.

5. **Put yourself in their shoes:** Empathy is a vital talent in sales, and salespeople who can put themselves in the customer's shoes may better

comprehend their wants and aspirations. This insight may allow salespeople to propose more relevant and beneficial solutions to the client.

By knowing the customer's demands, salespeople may provide solutions that deliver value and satisfy their requirements. This knowledge also helps to create trust and rapport with clients, leading to long-lasting connections.

Building trust

Building trust is one of the most crucial methods in marketing. Customers are more inclined to purchase from salespeople they trust, and creating trust needs a mix of abilities, attitudes, and actions. Here are some recommendations on how to create trust with customers:

1. **Be honest and transparent:** Honesty and openness are key to developing

trust. Salespeople should be straightforward about their goods and services, price, and any restrictions or obstacles the consumer may have while utilizing them.

2. **Listen actively:** Active listening is vital to creating trust. Salespeople should pay attention to customers' wants, worries, and desires and answer properly to create rapport.

3. **Be knowledgeable:** Salespeople who are educated about their goods, services, and industry are more likely to develop trust with consumers. This expertise allows them to deliver accurate and valuable information to consumers, gain trust, and position themselves as experts in their sector.

4. **Follow through on commitments:** When salespeople make promises to consumers, they must follow through

on them. This follow-through establishes trust and credibility and tells customers that the salesman appreciates their company and is devoted to their success.

5. **Empathize with customers:** Empathy is crucial to developing trust. Salespeople who can understand and empathize with their customer's wants, aspirations, and issues are more likely to create strong, enduring relationships with them.

6. **Provide outstanding service:** Providing exceptional service is vital to creating trust. Salespeople who go above and beyond to serve clients, give unique solutions, and provide continuing support are likelier to create strong, enduring connections with them.

In summary, developing trust is a vital skill in selling. Salespeople may develop trust by being honest and upfront, listening actively, being educated, following through on commitments, empathizing with clients, and offering outstanding service. By creating trust, salespeople may position themselves as trusted consultants to their consumers and form long-lasting partnerships that benefit both sides.

Creating a connection

Creating a connection is a key method in selling that entails creating rapport and establishing a relationship with the consumer. When salespeople can connect with the client, they are more likely to build trust, understand the customer's requirements, and give solutions suited to their circumstances. Here are some recommendations on how to develop a relationship with customers:

1. **exhibit real interest:** Salespeople should exhibit genuine interest in the customer's requirements, aspirations, and difficulties. This curiosity may assist in developing rapport and establishing a connection with the consumer.

2. **Ask personal inquiries:** Personal questions may help salespeople better understand the consumer. This insight may allow salespeople to give solutions more focused on the customer's demands.

3. **Use humor:** Humor may be an excellent method to break the ice and develop client relationships. Salespeople should utilize humor correctly and in a manner that resonates with the customer's personality and communication style.

4. **Share personal tales:** Sharing personal stories will enable salespeople to create consumer relationships. These anecdotes may build common ground and generate a relationship between the salesperson and the consumer.

5. **Discover shared interests:** Salespeople should strive to discover common interests with consumers. This similar interest helps create rapport and establish a connection with the consumer.

6. **Use active listening:** Active listening is vital to developing a relationship with clients. Salespeople should pay attention to the customer's words, tone, and body language to better understand their wants and goals.

By developing a relationship with clients, salespeople may create rapport, generate trust, and provide solutions

Resolving objections

Resolving objections is a fundamental approach to selling. Objections are ubiquitous in sales, and salespeople must be ready to answer them effectively to complete transactions successfully. Resolving objections entails listening to the customer's issues, understanding their viewpoint, and delivering solutions to their objections. Here are some pointers on how to address concerns in sales:

1. **Listen actively:** Salespeople should listen aggressively to the customer's arguments. They should allow consumers to voice their problems and ask clarifying questions to grasp their complaints better.

2. **Acknowledge the complaint:** Salespeople should acknowledge the customer's objection and indicate that they understand their worries. This recognition helps create rapport and trust with the consumer.

3. **Clarify the objection:** Salespeople should clarify the issue to ensure that they completely comprehend the customer's viewpoint. This explanation may allow salespeople to give tailored solutions that meet customers' needs.

4. **present a solution:** Salespeople should present a solution that solves the customer's concern. This solution should be personalized to the client's needs and concerns and deliver value to the consumer.

5. **express empathy:** Salespeople should empathize with the customer's

concerns. They should show that they understand the customer's viewpoint and are devoted to finding a solution to fulfilling their demands.

6. **Provide social evidence:** Social proof, such as customer testimonials or case studies, may effectively counter issues. Salespeople might utilize social proof to illustrate that their goods or services have helped other consumers overcome similar concerns.

By handling objections efficiently, salespeople may create trust, show their knowledge, and boost the probability of making a transaction. Salespeople should be prepared to handle objections and proactively present solutions that fulfill customers ' wants and concerns.

Customer Segmentation

Client segmentation is breaking a client base into smaller groups or segments based on certain criteria such as demographics, behavior, location, psychographics, or buying habits. This helps organizations adjust their marketing and sales efforts to each group's individual requirements and preferences, eventually leading to enhanced customer satisfaction and loyalty.

Various methods exist to segment clients based on the business, product or service, and other criteria. Here are a few examples of typical segmentation methods:

1. **Demographic segmentation:** Dividing clients based on criteria such as age, gender, income, education, and employment.

2. **Behavioral segmentation:** Dividing clients based on their purchasing

behavior, such as frequency of purchase, brand loyalty, and purchase history.

3. **Geographic segmentation:** Dividing clients depending on their location, such as nation, region, city, or zip code.

4. **Psychographic segmentation:** Dividing clients based on their personality characteristics, values, interests, and lifestyle.

5. **Firmographic segmentation:** Dividing consumers depending on the characteristics of their company, such as industry, size, revenue, and the number of people.

By segmenting consumers in these ways, organizations may focus their marketing efforts more effectively, produce more tailored goods and services, and ultimately form deeper connections with their customers.

The Customer Journey

The customer journey is a valuable framework for understanding customers' experiences and wants. It refers to the route a consumer follows from the first awareness of your product or service to the ultimate decision to buy and beyond. By mapping out the distinct phases of the customer journey, organizations may obtain insights into how their consumers think, feel, and act at each step and use this knowledge to enhance their marketing, sales, and customer service operations.

Here are the usual phases of the client journey:

1. **Awareness:** The consumer knows about your product or service via

numerous avenues such as advertising, social media, or word of mouth.

2. **Consideration:** The buyer begins to investigate and examine your product or service, comparing it with alternative possibilities.

3. **choice:** The consumer chooses to acquire your goods or service.

4. **Purchase:** The consumer completes the online or in-store purchase.

5. **Post-purchase:** The consumer utilizes your product or service and reviews their experience, which might impact their propensity to become a repeat customer or suggest others to your company.

By understanding the customer journey, organizations may find pain spots, chances for development, and places where they can give extra value to their consumers. This leads to enhanced client happiness, loyalty, and income.

CHAPTER THREE

The Power of Storytelling

Storytelling can be a successful strategy for marketing goods or services because it connects with people emotionally and helps them see themselves utilizing the product or service in their own life. When a seller shares a narrative that connects with a prospective consumer, they are more likely to remember the product or service and feel encouraged to take action.

Here are a few ways in which storytelling may be utilized as a selling technique:

1. **Creating an emotional connection:** Stories have the potential to delve into our emotions and make us feel something. When a salesperson

delivers a narrative that connects with a prospective consumer, it builds an emotional connection between them and the product or service.

2. **Demonstrating value:** By sharing tales about how a product or service has benefited others, a seller may illustrate the worth of the offering. Hearing about its great influence on someone else may be a strong incentive for prospective buyers.

3. **Painting a picture:** Stories help vendors to construct a realistic image of how a product or service may fit into a customer's life. By presenting particular situations and use cases, a seller may assist a prospective consumer see themselves using the product or service and experiencing the advantages.

4. **Building trust:** When a seller presents a tale that is honest and genuine, it may assist in developing trust with a possible consumer. People are more inclined to purchase from someone they trust, and sharing personal or relevant experiences may help develop that trust.

Overall, storytelling may be an effective selling method because it connects prospective consumers emotionally, emphasizes the item's value, draws a picture of how it might fit into their lives, and helps establish trust.

The Science of Storytelling

The science of storytelling in selling strategy is founded on the premise that our brains are built to react to tales. Studies have shown that when we hear a tale, our brains produce oxytocin, a hormone connected with trust and empathy, which might enhance our chance to interact with the narrative and remember it.

Here are a few ways in which the science of storytelling might be employed in marketing techniques:

Emphasizing the emotional impact

Emphasizing the emotional effect of a product or service via storytelling is a powerful method to engage prospective clients and create a memorable experience. By delivering tales that provoke emotions such as pleasure, grief, or surprise, a seller may help the prospective buyer connect with the product or service on a deeper level. Here are some instances of how emotional impact may be highlighted in storytelling as a marketing technique:

1. **Example of stressing happiness:** If a seller is selling a fitness program, they may relate a story of a client who began using the program and experienced a boost in confidence and happiness as they accomplished their fitness objectives. The tale might stress the emotional benefit of feeling more secure and comfortable in one's skin, which can motivate prospective clients to buy the fitness program.

2. **Example of stressing sadness:** If a vendor is marketing a charity or non-profit, they may share a tale of a person or community in need that has benefitted from the organization's efforts. The tale might stress the emotional impact of the hardship that the individual or community was experiencing and how the organization was able to assist relieve that suffering. This may develop an emotional connection with prospective

contributors and inspire them to give to the cause.

3. **Example of stressing surprise:** If a seller sells a new and innovative product, they may tell a narrative about the product's production and the startling discoveries made throughout the creation process. The tale may underline the emotional effect of the joy and surprise that comes from finding something new and innovative, which can drive prospective buyers to purchase the product.

Overall, accentuating the emotional effect of a product or service via storytelling is a powerful method to engage prospective consumers and create a memorable experience. By employing tales that generate emotions such as delight, grief, or surprise, a seller may develop an emotional connection with the prospective consumer and drive them to take action.

Using relevant characters

Utilizing sympathetic characters in storytelling is a strong method to develop a connection with prospective consumers and help them imagine themselves utilizing the product or service being offered. When consumers can relate to the characters in a tale, they become more involved with the narrative and are more likely to recall the offered product or service. Here are some instances of how relatable characters may be utilized in storytelling as a selling technique:

1. **Example of employing relatable characters in a personal anecdote:** If a seller sells a skincare product, they may share a personal narrative about how they suffered from acne or dry skin and how the skincare product helped improve their complexion. By

offering a meaningful personal narrative, the vendor may develop a connection with prospective clients who have similar skincare issues and drive them to buy the product.

2. **Example of using relatable characters in a customer success story:** If a seller is selling a productivity app, they can tell a story about how one of their customers, who is a busy entrepreneur or student, was able to achieve their goals and manage their time more effectively with the app. By adopting a relevant persona that prospective buyers can relate to, the seller may generate a feeling of trust and confidence in the goods.

3. **Example of employing relevant people in a case study:** If a salesperson sells a financial planning service, they may share a narrative

about how they assisted a family with comparable financial difficulties to reach their financial objectives. By utilizing sympathetic characters that prospective clients may empathize with, the seller can build trust and confidence in their financial planning services.

Overall, utilizing sympathetic characters in storytelling is a strong method to develop a connection with prospective consumers and help them imagine themselves using the product or service being offered. By employing personal anecdotes, customer success stories, or case studies featuring sympathetic people, a seller may build trust and confidence in their product or service and drive prospective buyers to take action.

Creating a narrative arc

Creating a narrative arc in storytelling is a strong approach to engaging prospective consumers and helping them recognize the value of the offered product or service. By framing the tale in a style that follows a classic narrative arc, with a beginning, middle, and finish, a seller may generate momentum and suspense that catches the audience's attention and pushes them to take action. Here are some instances of how establishing a narrative arc may be utilized in storytelling as a selling technique:

1. **Example of establishing a narrative arc in a product demonstration:** If a salesperson presents a new kitchen gadget, they may establish a narrative arc by beginning with a problem or obstacle many home chefs confront, such as trying to cut vegetables quickly and effectively. They may then propose the device as the answer to

this difficulty, illustrating how it can make the cooking process simpler and more fun. By organizing the presentation this way, the vendor may generate a feeling of tension and resolve that pushes prospective clients to acquire the item.

2. **Example of creating a narrative arc in a customer success story:** If a seller is selling a weight loss program, they can create a narrative arc by starting with the customer's initial struggle with weight loss, then introducing the program as the solution to their problem, and finally showing how the customer achieved their weight loss goals and transformed their life. By arranging the tale this way, the salesperson may generate a feeling of momentum and drive among prospective consumers battling similar issues.

3. **Example of building a narrative arc in a case study:** If a seller is selling a marketing service, they can create a narrative arc by starting with the client's initial challenge, such as struggling to attract new customers, then introducing the marketing service as the solution to their problem, and finally showing how the client achieved their marketing goals and grew their business. By organizing the case study in this manner, the seller may generate a feeling of trust and competence in their marketing services.

Overall, building a narrative arc in storytelling is a strong approach to engaging prospective consumers and helping them recognize the product's or service's value. By framing the tale following a classic narrative arc, a seller may generate a feeling of momentum, suspense, and conclusion that drives prospective buyers to take action.

Using visual aids

Using visual aids is a robust approach to increasing narrative in a selling strategy.

Visual aids like photographs, films, and diagrams may assist in reinforcing the point being delivered by the narrative and make it more memorable and compelling for prospective buyers. Here are some instances of how visual aids may be employed in storytelling as a selling technique:

1. **Example of employing visual aids in a product demonstration:** If a seller is exhibiting a new software product, they may use visual aids such as screenshots and videos to illustrate how the product works and its important features. By employing

visual aids, the seller may enrich the tale and assist prospective buyers in grasping the value of the offered product.

2. **Example of employing visual aids in a customer success story:** If a seller is selling a skincare product, they may include before-and-after photographs to highlight the change that a client experienced after using the product. By adding visual aids, the seller may generate a more dramatic and emotional effect on prospective clients and highlight the product's advantages.

3. **Example of employing visual aids in a case study:** If a seller offers a financial planning service, they may use diagrams and charts to explain how their service can assist customers in accomplishing their financial objectives. By adding visual aids, the

vendor may clarify complicated ideas and make them more accessible to prospective clients.

Overall, integrating visual aids in storytelling is a great approach to strengthen the selling strategy and make the tale more engaging and memorable for prospective buyers. By employing visual aids like photographs, videos, and diagrams, a seller can create a more immersive and engaging experience that reinforces the message and helps prospective buyers grasp the value of the product or service being offered.

Using Storytelling in Sales

Using storytelling in sales is a strong approach that may help salespeople connect with prospective customers, create trust and rapport, and ultimately complete more transactions. Here are some strategies for utilizing narrative in sales:

1. **Understand your audience:** To write a successful sales narrative, you must understand your target and their wants, pain areas, and objectives. This will help you develop a tale that connects with them and explains how your product or service can solve their issues and help them reach their objectives.

2. **Keep it basic and brief:** Your sales narrative should be straightforward and concise, with a clear beginning, middle, and finish. Avoid using technical jargon or sophisticated terminology that may confuse or overwhelm your readers. Keep the emphasis on the core message of your tale and how it connects to your product or service.

3. **Use relevant characters:** Using relatable characters in your sales tale will help your audience connect with your message and see themselves in the story. This may generate an emotional connection and develop trust and rapport with prospective consumers.

4. **Use visual aids:** Visual aids like photographs, videos, and diagrams may assist to improve your sales narrative and make it more compelling and memorable. Use visual aids related to your message and underline the advantages of your product or service.

5. **Use a narrative arc:** Using it in your sales story may generate momentum and suspense that engages your audience and drives them to take action. Start with an issue or difficulty your audience can connect to,

promote your product or service as the answer, and illustrate how it can help them reach their objectives.

Overall, employing storytelling in sales may be a strong strategy to create trust and connection with prospective clients and eventually complete more transactions. By writing a captivating sales narrative that connects with your audience and showcases the value of your product or service, you can build an emotional connection and drive prospective buyers to take action.

Crafting a Compelling Sales Narrative

Crafting a captivating sales story is crucial to engaging prospective clients, developing rapport, and completing more purchases.

Here are some strategies for developing an engaging sales narrative:

1. **Start with a powerful introduction:** Your opener should attract your audience's attention and set the scene for your tale. Use a hook or an attention-grabbing phrase to lure your audience in and stimulate their curiosity.

2. **Identify the issue:** Clearly define the difficulty that your prospective clients are experiencing. This helps your audience connect to the tale and comprehend the context of your product or service.

3. **propose your solution:** After identifying the issue, propose your answer. Explain how your product or service addresses the issue and improves your client's lives.

4. **Use social evidence:** Social proof is a strong technique to establish credibility and generate trust. Use instances of how your product or service has benefited others, such as customer testimonials or case studies.

5. **Focus on the advantages:** Instead of merely outlining the qualities of your product or service, focus on the benefits. Please explain how your solution can enhance your consumers' lives and help them attain their objectives.

6. **Use a clear call to action:** Your story should finish with a clear call to action. Encourage your audience to take the next step, whether arranging a demo or completing a purchase.

7. **Practice, practice:** Finally, rehearse your sales story. Please ensure you're

comfortable with the narrative and can deliver it naturally and confidently.

Overall, building a captivating sales story takes time and work, but engaging prospective customers and completing more purchases may pay off in a major manner. By concentrating on the issue, solution, advantages, and social proof and employing a clear call to action, you can construct a sales story that connects with your audience and drives them to take action.

CHAPTER FOUR

Building Trust and Credibility

Building trust and credibility is a crucial selling tactic that may help you develop strong and long-lasting connections with your consumers. Here are some successful techniques to create trust and credibility:

1. **Be upfront:** Being honest with your consumers about your goods, services, and procedures is vital in developing trust. Provide honest and accurate information and be clear about any restrictions or obstacles.

2. **Demonstrate expertise:** Customers want to deal with individuals that are informed and experienced in their

sector. Please share your knowledge by giving important insights and answers to their difficulties.

3. **Provide social evidence:** Social proof, such as testimonials, case studies, and reviews, may assist develop credibility and trust with prospective consumers. Share good comments from your current clients to illustrate your capacity to generate superior outcomes.

4. **Build relationships:** Building a personal connection with your consumers may assist build trust and loyalty. Take the time to learn their wants, preferences, and ambitions, and personalize your solutions to match their requirements.

5. **Be responsive:** Attention to consumer enquiries and concerns is crucial in developing confidence.

Respond immediately and courteously to any inquiries or difficulties that occur and exhibit your dedication to delivering outstanding customer service.

Overall, creating trust and credibility involves a continual effort to prioritize the demands and interests of your consumers. By showing transparency, knowledge, social proof, relationship-building, and responsiveness, you may develop a solid trust foundation that can drive sales and company success.

The Psychology of Trust in Sales

The psychology of trust in sales is founded on the concept that consumers are more willing to conduct business with persons or firms they trust. Many elements, such as honesty, competency, dependability, consistency, and empathy, create trust.

Here are some significant psychological characteristics that impact trust in sales:

Social Proof

Social proof is a psychological concept that outlines how individuals are affected by the acts and attitudes of others, especially those in their social circles or those they see as being similar to themselves. Social proof may be a strong tool for creating trust and credibility with prospective clients in sales.

When consumers are unsure about a product or service, they typically resort to the views and experiences of others to aid their decision-making process. If consumers perceive that others have had great experiences with a certain product or service, they are more inclined to trust and be ready to try it themselves.

There are various ways that social proof may be utilized in sales:

1. **Customer testimonials:** Sharing testimonials from delighted customers may be a powerful method to illustrate the value of a product or service. When prospective consumers see that others have had excellent experiences with a product or service, they are more inclined to believe that it will also work for them.

2. **Influencer endorsements:** Influencers and celebrities may also be strong sources of social proof. When someone with a huge following promotes a product or service, their followers are more inclined to trust and be ready to try it.

3. **Social media analytics:** Social media metrics such as likes, shares, and followers may also be social proof. When prospective buyers realize that a product or service has a huge

following on social media, they are more inclined to trust it and be ready to try it.

4. **Expert reviews:** Reviews from specialists in a subject may also be social proof. When prospective consumers realize that a product or service has been evaluated and suggested by experts in the area, they are more inclined to trust and try it.

Social proof may be a great strategy for creating trust and credibility with prospective clients. By proving that others have had great experiences with a product or service, companies may improve the possibility that future consumers would be willing to give it a try themselves.

Reciprocity

Reciprocity is a psychological term that expresses the human urge to react to a good deed with another positive action. In sales, reciprocity may be a great technique for creating trust and credibility with prospective consumers.

When a company delivers something of value to a prospective client without expecting anything in return, the potential customer may experience a feeling of obligation and be more inclined to reciprocate by making a purchase or doing some other positive action. People naturally want to balance the scales and avoid feeling like they are in debt to others.

There are various ways that reciprocity may be employed in sales:

1. **Free samples:** Offering free samples of a product may be a robust approach to induce the reciprocity effect. When prospective consumers get something of value for free, they may feel forced to repay by making a

purchase or promoting the product to others.

2. **Gifts:** Providing gifts or incentives to prospective consumers may help activate the reciprocity effect. When prospective consumers get a present or incentive, they may feel more likely to reciprocate by making a purchase or doing other positive actions.

3. **Useful advice:** Providing advice or information to prospective clients activates reciprocity. When prospective clients get beneficial information without being asked to pay for it, they may feel more motivated to reciprocate by purchasing or performing some other positive action.

Reciprocity may be a great technique for creating trust and credibility with prospective clients. By delivering something of value without expecting anything in return, companies may activate the reciprocity effect and raise the possibility that prospective consumers will be inclined to purchase or take other positive actions.

Consistency

Consistency is a psychological term emphasizing the human desire to act in ways consistent with our prior behaviors, attitudes, and beliefs. In the sales context, consistency may be important for creating trust and credibility with prospective consumers.

When a firm is consistent in its language and behavior, prospective consumers are more likely to trust and be willing to purchase. This is because people naturally need stability and predictability and tend to perceive consistent conduct as a sign of dependability and credibility.

There are various ways that consistency may be employed in sales:

1. **Consistent message:** Ensuring that all messaging and branding are consistent across all platforms will assist in developing trust and credibility with prospective consumers. When prospective consumers see the same message and branding across a firm's website, social media platforms, and advertising, they are more likely to trust the business and regard it as reputable and legitimate.

2. **Consistent quality:** Ensuring that the quality of goods or services is consistent may also help to create confidence and credibility with prospective consumers. When consumers know that they can anticipate the same level of quality every time they make a purchase, they are more inclined to trust the

company and be ready to make repeat purchases.

3. **Consistent follow-up:** Following up frequently with prospective clients may also assist in creating trust and credibility. When a firm follows up with prospective consumers promptly and regularly, it indicates that the business is dependable and cares about their requirements.

Consistency may be an effective strategy for creating confidence and credibility with prospective clients. By displaying a consistent message, quality, and follow-up, companies may raise the possibility that prospective consumers would be eager to purchase and become repeat customers.

Authority

Authority is a psychological term that expresses the human predisposition to respect and trust persons who are viewed as competent and experienced in a given subject. In sales, an authority may be valuable for developing trust and credibility with prospective consumers.

When a firm is able to establish its authority in a certain subject, prospective clients are more likely to trust it and be eager to make a purchase. This is because people naturally tend to defer to others viewed as experts in a certain field.

There are various ways that authority may be employed in sales:

1. **Expert endorsements:** Endorsements from specialists in a given subject may be a powerful method to display authority. When prospective consumers realize that a well-respected expert in the industry has approved a product or service,

they are more likely to trust it and be inclined to make a purchase.

2.   **Industry awards**: Industry awards and accolades may also be a great approach to display authority. When prospective clients realize that a firm has gained honors or recognition in its area, they are more inclined to trust it and regard it as a leader in the field.

3.   **Thought leadership:** Demonstrating thought leadership via material like blog articles, white papers, and webinars may also assist to develop authority. When prospective consumers realize that a firm is providing quality material and sharing its knowledge in a certain area, they are more inclined to trust it and regard it as an authority.

Authority may be valuable for developing trust and credibility with prospective consumers. By displaying knowledge and thought leadership in a certain field, companies may raise the possibility that prospective consumers would be eager to make a purchase and become loyal customers.

Empathy

Empathy is a psychological term that represents the capacity to comprehend and share the experiences and viewpoints of others. In the context of sales, empathy may be a valuable tool for creating trust and credibility with prospective consumers.

When a firm can empathize with prospective clients, they are more likely to trust it and be eager to purchase. This is because people have a natural urge to connect with others on an emotional level and tend to be more eager to conduct business with persons or firms that display empathy and understanding.

There are various ways that empathy may be employed in sales:

1. **Active listening:** entails concentrating on what a prospective consumer says and proving that you understand and care about their worries. Organizations may display empathy and create trust by carefully listening to prospective clients.

2. **Personalization:** Personalizing the sales experience to fit each consumer's distinct requirements and concerns may also display empathy. When prospective consumers believe a firm is considering its unique requirements, they are more likely to trust it and be inclined to purchase.

3. **Understanding pain points:** Understanding prospective clients' pain points and obstacles may help

display empathy. When a firm can demonstrate that it understands the issues that prospective consumers are having and can provide answers, it may develop trust and credibility.

Empathy may be a great strategy for creating trust and credibility with prospective clients. By displaying active listening, customization, and a knowledge of pain issues, companies may raise the possibility that prospective consumers would be eager to purchase and become loyal customers.

Establishing Credibility with Prospects In sales

Establishing credibility is essential to the sales process as it allows prospects to trust you and your product or service. Here are some techniques to develop credibility with your prospects:

Develop a strong web presence

Developing a solid online presence is a critical component of effective sales nowadays. Here are some actions you may take to develop and maintain a strong internet presence:

1. **Create a professional website:** Your website should be aesthetically attractive, simple to use, and should promote your goods or services. Ensure it is optimized for search engines so that prospective clients can quickly discover you online.

2. **Use social media:** Social media is a wonderful tool for creating connections and interacting with prospective consumers. Identify the social media sites where your target audience is most engaged and

develop interesting content highlighting your expertise and goods or services.

3. **Publish valuable content:** Establish yourself as a thought leader in your area by releasing blog posts, articles, videos, or podcasts that give helpful advice and insights to your target audience. This will assist in developing trust and credibility with prospective consumers.

4. **Utilize email marketing:** Use email marketing campaigns to nurture leads and keep your consumers updated about new goods or services, specials, and other pertinent information.

5. **react to online reviews:** Monitor and react to reviews on Google, Yelp, and other relevant sites. Responding to reviews, even negative ones,

indicates that you appreciate customer input and are devoted to delivering outstanding service.

6. **Network online:** Join online forums, organizations, and associations related to your sector and connect with other members. This can help you form connections and enhance your reputation as a competent and helpful expert in your sector.

Remember, a great online presence requires time and work but is worth the investment. Building a good online presence can attract new leads, generate trust and reputation, and eventually boost your sales.

Demonstrate knowledge

Demonstrating expertise is a crucial element of the sales process. Here are some strategies to properly display your expertise:

1. **Do your homework:** Before communicating with a prospect, take the time to investigate their company, industry, and pain issues. This will assist you in finding areas where you can provide value and show your expertise.

2. **Listen actively:** When talking with prospects, listen to their issues and ask questions to grasp their requirements better. This will convey that you are truly interested in helping them discover answers to their challenges.

3. **Share useful information:** Use your expertise and experience to deliver helpful insights and solutions to your prospects. Share relevant facts, case studies, or industry trends to support your suggestions.

4. **Be concise:** Avoid overloading your prospects with too much information. Instead, concentrate on delivering clear and concise answers that are easy to grasp.

5. **Use storytelling:** Tales or anecdotes to explain how your product or service has benefited other consumers in similar circumstances. This will assist in creating credibility and developing trust with your prospects.

6. **illustrate your competence:** Highlight your experience and certifications that illustrate your expertise in your sector. These are credentials, honors, or speaking engagements.

Remember, exhibiting expertise is not about showing off what you know but leveraging your knowledge to assist your prospects in solving their issues and accomplishing their objectives. By exhibiting your experience, you may create credibility and develop trust with your prospects, eventually leading to more effective sales.

Be genuine

Being genuine is a vital component of the sales process. Here are some methods to remain real while dealing with prospects:

1. **Be yourself:** Authenticity begins with being loyal to yourself. Please don't pretend to be someone you're not since this will make it tougher for prospects to trust you.

2. **Build rapport:** Building rapport with your prospects helps create a relationship and generate trust. Please get to know your prospects personally and demonstrate a genuine interest in their lives and enterprises.

3. **confess when you don't know something:** It's alright to confess when you don't know something. Be honest and straightforward, and demonstrate a desire to discover the solutions to your prospects' queries.

4. **Share your values:** Share your personal and professional values with potential prospects. This helps to create a common ground and develop trust.

5. **Focus on solutions:** Instead of attempting to sell anything, deliver answers to your prospects' issues. This implies that you are interested in assisting them rather than merely making a sale.

6. **Follow through:** Follow through on your pledges and commitments. This implies that you are reliable and trustworthy.

Remember, genuineness is not something that can be faked. It comes from being loyal to yourself and your principles and having a genuine interest in assisting your prospects. Being real can generate trust and build strong connections with your prospects, which is vital for effective sales.

Provide value

Providing value to your clients is vital for creating great connections and boosting sales. Here are some methods to give value to the sales process:

1. **Understand your consumers' needs:** Take the time to understand your customers' pain areas and demands. This will assist you in delivering solutions that solve their concerns and provide value.

2. **Be a problem-solver:** Focus on becoming a problem-solver for your consumers. Offer solutions that meet their individual requirements and assist them in reaching their objectives.

3. **Share insights and expertise:** Share your knowledge and expertise with your customers. Offer insights and suggestions that allow people to make educated choices and achieve better results.

4. **Offer outstanding customer service:** giving excellent customer service is vital to giving value. Be receptive to your client's wants and problems, and give timely and effective service.

5. **Provide continuing support:** Offer continual help to your customers, even after the deal has been made.

This displays that you are devoted to their achievement and helps to develop long-term partnerships.

6. **Provide other resources:** Provide additional resources, such as white papers, case studies, or instructional material that will enable your clients to reach their objectives.

Remember, giving value is not simply about selling items or services. It's about knowing your client's requirements and giving solutions that allow them to reach their objectives. You may create strong connections with your clients by giving value, leading to more successful sales over time.

Focus on results

Focusing on outcomes is vital in sales as it helps to drive success and develop long-term connections with your clients. Here are some approaches to concentrate on outcomes in the sales process:

1. **Set explicit goals:** Set clear objectives for each sales engagement, whether a phone call, email, or meeting. This will enable you to keep focused on the target objective and guarantee that you're working towards obtaining outcomes.

2. **Measure progress:** Measure your progress towards your goals often. This can enable you to find areas where you're performing well and places where you need to improve.

3. **Stay focused on the customer:** Stay focused on the customer's wants and ambitions. This will assist you in giving solutions that are connected with their aims and help them to get the outcomes they're searching for.

4. **Be proactive:** Identify and resolve any obstacles that might affect the outcomes. This entails anticipating concerns, preparing replies in advance, and finding areas where you can contribute value to drive outcomes.

5. **Deliver on your promises:** Deliver on your pledges and commitments to your Customers. This implies that you're loyal and trustworthy, which helps to develop great connections and promote repeat business.

6. **Measure and assess:** Measure and evaluate the success of your sales activities. This will assist you in determining what's working well and what needs improvement, so you can alter your strategy and concentrate on achieving greater outcomes.

Remember, concentrating on outcomes is about being proactive and customer-focused, and delivering on your commitments. Concentrating on results may create trust and credibility with your customers, which will assist in achieving effective sales outcomes over time.

Show social proof

Showing social proof is a robust approach to developing credibility and trust with your prospects and consumers. Here are some strategies to include social proof in your sales process:

1. **Use client testimonials:** Gather testimonials from delighted customers and distribute them on your website, social media platforms, or sales presentations. These testimonials illustrate the value of your goods or services and give social evidence that

others have had a great experience working with you.

2. **Share case studies:** Share case studies that demonstrate how your goods or services have helped other consumers reach their objectives. These case studies give real-world examples of your competencies and assist in establishing your experience and trustworthiness.

3. **Highlight customer reviews:** Highlight favorable customer reviews on your website, social media platforms, or other marketing materials. These evaluations give honest feedback and assist in creating confidence with future clients.

4. **Use industry recognition:** Incorporate this in your marketing materials if your firm has won industry honors or recognition. This helps to

develop credibility and indicates that you're a trustworthy and acknowledged supplier in your business.

5. **Show social media activity:** Show social media engagement and followers to indicate that you have a significant following and are trusted by others. The number of followers or likes on your social media sites or through social proof methods such as Klout ratings may indicate this.

Remember, social proof helps to develop credibility and trust with your prospects and consumers. By implementing social proof into your sales process, you can establish your knowledge and develop a solid reputation to promote effective sales results over time.

Communicate effectively In sales

Effective communication is vital in sales to develop relationships, understand customer requirements, and complete transactions. Here are some techniques to communicate successfully in sales:

1. **Listen actively:** Active listening entails paying attention to what the customer is saying, asking questions to clarify their demands, and showing that you understand their problems. This helps to create rapport and convey that you care about their requirements.

2. **Be precise and succinct:** Be straightforward and concise to prevent confusion or misunderstandings. Use straightforward language and avoid jargon or technical phrases the consumer may need help comprehending.

3. **Use stories:** Stories may assist in emphasizing your arguments and developing an emotional connection with the consumer. Use tales relevant to the customer's requirements and explain how your goods or services may help them reach their objectives.

4. **Build rapport:** Building rapport means building a relationship with the consumer via common interests, experiences, or ideals. This helps to create trust and establish a connection that may lead to effective sales results.

5. **Use visual aids:** Visual aids such as charts, graphs, or photographs may assist in expressing difficult information in a simple grasp. Use visual aids relevant to the customer's demands and assist in highlighting the value of your goods or services.

6. **Follow up:** Following up with consumers is vital to verify their requirements are being fulfilled and resolve any complaints or difficulties. This displays that you care about their needs and are devoted to their achievement.

Remember, good communication is about creating connections, understanding your customer's requirements, and showcasing the value of your products or services. Communicating effectively may create trust and credibility with your consumers and achieve successful sales results over time.

Navigating Objections and Concerns

Objections and worries are a normal part of the sales process, and how you negotiate them may make all the difference in completing a purchase. Here are some techniques for handling objections and concerns:

1. **Listen actively:** When a consumer expresses criticism or worry, listen attentively to what they're saying. Please don't interrupt or attempt to persuade them that they're incorrect. Instead, ask questions to explain their issues and indicate that you understand their viewpoint.

2. **recognize the complaint:** Once you've listened to the customer's problem, recognize it. This implies that you take their problems seriously and are determined to resolve them.

3. **Provide solutions:** Provide solutions that solve the customer's problems. This can entail giving new information, offering an alternative product or service, or modifying the terms of the

contract to fit their requirements better.

4. **Use social proof:** Social evidence may be an effective approach to answering objections and concerns. Share testimonials, case studies, or other examples illustrating how your goods or services have helped other customers solve similar difficulties.

5. **remain optimistic:** When addressing objections and concerns, it's crucial to remain positive and focused on finding solutions. Avoid being defensive or aggressive since this might destroy your connection with the consumer.

6. **Follow up:** After resolving objections and concerns, follow up with the client to confirm that their requirements are being addressed and to address any other issues that may develop.

Remember, objections and worries are a chance to display your knowledge and create confidence with the consumer. By listening actively, admitting issues, suggesting solutions, and being upbeat, you can effectively overcome objections and concerns and complete more business.

CHAPTER FIVE

Leveraging Technology and Data

Technology and data have become vital tools for firms to streamline their sales processes and improve performance. Here are some ways that firms might employ technology and data in sales:

1. **CRM Systems:** Customer Relationship Management (CRM) systems are software solutions that enable firms to manage their customer interactions and sales processes. An effective CRM system may give insights into consumer behavior, preferences, and purchase history. This data may be used to adapt sales and marketing efforts to particular

clients, boosting the probability of completing agreements and developing long-term connections.

2. **Sales Analytics:** Sales analytics solutions may give firms a greater insight into their sales performance, enabling them to discover areas for development and make data-driven choices. These systems may measure variables like revenue, sales cycle time, and conversion rates, offering insights into which methods are working and which are not.

3. **Marketing Automation:** Marketing automation solutions enable firms to automate repetitive marketing processes like email campaigns and social media postings. This may save sales teams time and effort while boosting their marketing activities' accuracy and efficacy.

4. AI-Powered Sales Tools: Artificial intelligence (AI) has become more essential in sales, with many organizations utilizing AI-powered tools to better their sales processes. AI may be used to analyze client data, forecast purchase behavior, and automate some sales duties, freeing up sales professionals to concentrate on more difficult jobs.

5. **Mobile Sales Tools:** Mobile technology has become a crucial tool for sales teams, enabling them to access client data and sales materials on the go. Mobile sales tools also allow sales staff to engage with customers more successfully by providing real-time information and enabling them to reply swiftly to consumer enquiries.

By embracing technology and data, organizations may get a competitive advantage in sales by enhancing their efficiency, accuracy, and effectiveness.

Using Data to Enhance Sales Performance

Data is a strong instrument that can be exploited to increase sales success in various ways. Here are some ways organizations may utilize data to better their sales efforts:

1. **Customer Segmentation:** By evaluating customer data, organizations may segment their client base into multiple groups depending on criteria such as demographics, habits, and purchasing patterns. This helps businesses to focus their sales and marketing efforts on certain demographics, boosting the efficacy of their approach.

2. **Sales Forecasting:** By collecting sales data over time, firms may build sales predictions that assist them in planning and allocating resources more efficiently. This helps businesses to improve their sales efforts and deploy resources more effectively.

3. **Performance recording:** By recording important sales indicators, firms may evaluate their sales performance and find areas for improvement. This helps them to change their sales methods and techniques to increase performance and obtain better outcomes.

4. **Sales Funnel Optimization:** By examining data on customer behavior at each step of the sales funnel, firms may discover places where consumers are falling off and modify

their sales funnel to boost conversion rates.

5. **Lead Scoring:** By utilizing data to score leads based on behavior, demographics, and engagement, organizations can prioritize their sales efforts and concentrate on the most promising possibilities.

Data is a great resource that may enable organizations to improve their sales efforts and achieve better outcomes. Organizations may obtain significant insights into consumer behavior and sales performance by employing data analytics tools and methodologies, enabling them to make data-driven choices and enhance their sales tactics.

Automation and Artificial Intelligence in Sales

Automation and artificial intelligence (AI) are becoming more significant in sales since they allow organizations to optimize operations, save time, and enhance overall performance. Here are some ways that organizations may leverage automation and AI in their sales efforts:

1. **Lead Scoring:** AI-powered lead scoring systems may assess data on consumer behavior, demographics, and engagement to provide scores to leads. This allows sales teams to concentrate their efforts and focus on the most potential offers.

2. **Sales Forecasting:** AI algorithms can examine past sales data and industry trends to provide accurate sales projections, allowing firms to

plan and allocate resources more efficiently.

3. **Personalization:** AI may evaluate consumer data and develop customized sales pitches and marketing communications for each unique customer.

4. **Chatbots:** AI-powered chatbots may automate customer care interactions, giving consumers rapid and accurate replies to their enquiries and decreasing the pressure on sales agents.

5. **Sales Process Automation:** Automation solutions may automate repetitive sales operations, such as data input and lead qualifying, freeing sales representatives to concentrate on more complicated duties.

Overall, automation and AI enable firms to enhance their sales performance and achieve better outcomes by reducing operations, boosting efficiency, and enhancing the customer experience. By embracing these technologies, organizations may acquire a competitive advantage in the industry and achieve more success in their sales operations.

CHAPTER SIX

Developing Your Sales Process

Developing a sales process is vital for every firm that wants to raise revenue and develop. A sales process is a systematic approach to selling that describes the actions a salesperson should follow to clinch a contract. Here are some stages to take to establish your sales process:

1. **Identify your target audience:** You need to know who your ideal client is, their wants and pain points, and what drives them to purchase.

2. **Define your sales funnel:** A sales funnel visualizes a prospect's stages to becoming a client. Your sales

should cover the steps of the purchasing process, from lead creation through completing the deal.

3. **Determine your sales cycle:** A sales cycle is when a prospect travels through your sales funnel. Understanding your sales cycle can help you establish realistic sales objectives and identify how many prospects you need to produce to meet those targets.

4. **Create a lead creation strategy:** You need to plan to produce leads that fit your target population. This might involve content marketing, email marketing, social media, and paid advertising.

5. **Develop a sales script:** A sales script is a written plan of the discussion you conduct with a prospect. It should

contain the questions you ask to identify their requirements, concerns they may have, and the advantages of your product or service.

6. **teach your sales team:** Once you have a sales process in place, you need to teach your sales staff the process, the script, and the resources they need to be successful.

7. **Monitor and modify your process:** Your sales process is not fixed in stone. You need to routinely assess the outcomes of your sales process and adjust it based on what works and what doesn't.

Remember, a sales process is not a one-size-fits-all answer. You must adapt your procedure to meet your company and target audience. By following these steps, you can design a sales process that will help you boost income and expand your firm.

The Fundamentals of Sales Process Design

Sales process design is the art and science of building a sales process that is successful, efficient, and repeatable. Here are some important ideas to bear in mind while creating a sales process:

1. **Start with the goal:** The first stage in building a sales process is establishing the intended result. What do you wish to achieve? What is the purpose of your sales process? The answers to these questions will inform the design of your method.

2. **Understand your buyer's journey:** You need to understand your

customers' path while purchasing. This will help you build a sales process consistent with their requirements and expectations.

3. **Define the stages of your sales:** A sales process comprises stages, each with its own set of actions, objectives, and results. Define the steps of your sales process and the actions that need to happen at each level.

4. **Develop a sales playbook:** A sales playbook is a document that explains the sales process, the buyer's journey, the phases of the sales, and the precise actions that need to happen at each level. It should also incorporate best practices, scripts, objection management, and other tools to assist sales professionals complete transactions.

5. **Automate your sales process:** Technology may assist in simplifying and automating many of the operations in your sales process, such as lead scoring, lead nurturing, and follow-up. Look for technologies that may help you automate these procedures to save time and enhance efficiency.

6. **Train your sales team:** A sales process is only successful if your sales staff understands it and knows how to apply it. Train your sales staff on the sales process, the sales playbook, and the tools they need to be successful.

7. **Monitor and enhance your sales process:** Your sales process is not fixed in stone. You need to evaluate the outcomes of your sales process and adjust it based on what works and what doesn't.

By following these essential principles, you can develop a sales process that is successful, efficient, and repeatable. Remember, the key to a successful sales process is to connect it with your buyers' requirements and expectations and continually improve it based on feedback and outcomes.

Identifying Key Sales Metrics

Finding essential sales metrics is critical for analyzing the performance of your sales process and finding opportunities for improvement. Here are some critical sales KPIs to consider:

1. **Sales revenue:** This is the overall income earned through sales. It is the most crucial statistic for assessing the performance of your sales process.

2. **Sales growth:** This indicator reflects the increase in sales revenue over a given period. It helps you evaluate if your sales process is producing growth or not.

3. **Sales conversion rate:** This indicator counts the proportion of leads that turn into customers. It helps you assess how efficiently your sales process turns leads into clients.

4. **Average deal size:** This indicator gauges the average size of your sales transactions. It helps you realize the value of each sale and the possibility for development.

5. **Sales cycle duration:** This indicator measures the time it takes for a lead to become a client. It helps you analyze how long it takes to complete

business and discover areas where you can improve your sales process.

6. **Sales pipeline:** This indicator represents the overall value of all the transactions in your sales pipeline. It helps you grasp the potential money that might be made.

7. **client acquisition cost (CAC):** This statistic estimates the cost of obtaining a new client. It helps you understand how much it costs to gain new consumers and discover areas where you may minimize expenditures.

8. **Customer lifetime value (CLTV):** This statistic evaluates the overall worth of a customer over the whole duration of their association with your firm. It helps you assess the potential worth of each client and prioritize customer retention activities.

By measuring these critical sales indicators, you may acquire a better insight into the success of your sales process and find areas where you can improve. Remember, the key to a successful sales process is consistently analyzing and adjusting your KPIs to accomplish your sales objectives.

Sales Forecasting and Pipeline Management

Sales forecasting and pipeline management are two critical components of a successful sales strategy. Sales forecasting includes estimating future sales based on historical performance, market trends, and other variables. Pipeline management refers to managing the many phases of the sales process, from lead creation to completing agreements.

Sales forecasting may be done in several methods, including historical analysis, market research, and consumer surveys. It is vital to employ a variety of strategies to guarantee accurate forecasts. By effectively estimating sales, firms may make educated choices regarding inventory, workforce, and other resources.

Pipeline management entails keeping track of leads and sales prospects and moving them through the sales process. This may entail employing a customer relationship management (CRM) system to monitor client interactions and define objectives and targets for sales reps.

Effective pipeline management may help organizations discover bottlenecks in the sales process and change their strategy appropriately. It also helps salespeople concentrate their efforts and focus on the most promising prospects.

Sales forecasting and pipeline management are critical components of a successful sales strategy. Organizations may maximize their resources and boost their bottom line by properly projecting future sales and successfully managing the sales process.

CHAPTER SEVEN

Effective Communication in Sales

Effective communication is vital in sales since it helps you to connect with your consumers, understand their requirements, and develop trust. Here are some ideas for good communication in sales:

1. **Be straightforward and concise:** Use basic, easy-to-understand language and avoid technical jargon that may confuse your consumers. Be succinct and get to the point immediately.

2. **Listen actively:** Listen to your consumers to understand their requirements and worries. Ask

open-ended inquiries to encourage them to offer additional information.

3. **Use empathy:** Put yourself in your customer's shoes and comprehend their viewpoint. This might help you personalize your pitch to their demands and create rapport.

4. **exhibit confidence:** Speak confidently and confidently to exhibit your knowledge and develop credibility with your customers.

5. **Use visual aids:** Visual aids such as diagrams or charts to assist in straightforwardly presenting detailed information.

6. **Practice active engagement:** Engage your consumers throughout the sales process. Acknowledge their worries, answer their inquiries, and show them you listen.

7. Follow up with your consumers after the transaction to guarantee their pleasure and develop a long-term connection.

Adopting these tactics allows you to interact successfully with your consumers and boost your sales performance. Remember that good communication is a two-way street; therefore, listening attentively and changing your approach depending on your customer's wants and concerns is crucial.

Active Listening and Questioning Techniques

Active listening and questioning tactics are key to successful communication, especially in sales. Here are some ways to active listening and successful questioning:

Active Listening Techniques:

1. **Give your undivided attention:** Focus on the person speaking and give them your full attention. Avoid multitasking or distractions.

2. **Use nonverbal signs:** Use nonverbal cues like nodding, keeping eye contact, and leaning in to demonstrate that you are attentively listening.

3. **Paraphrase:** Repeat what you have heard in your own words to check that you have received it properly.

4. **Clarify:** Ask clarifying questions to ensure that you completely comprehend what the individual is saying.

5. **Empathize:** Put yourself in their position and attempt to comprehend their viewpoint.

Questioning Techniques:

1. **Open-ended inquiries:** Use open-ended questions to encourage the individual to share additional information and to create a better understanding of their needs and concerns.

2. **Closed-ended questions:** Use closed-ended questions for precise information, such as verifying a time or date.

3. **Leading questions:** Use leading questions to influence the discussion and urge the speaker to reveal additional information.

4. **Reflective questions:** Use reflective questions to urge individuals to think more thoroughly about their wants and problems.

5. **Hypothetical questions:** Use hypothetical questions to examine alternative answers and possibilities.

By employing these active listening and questioning strategies, you can develop a stronger connection with your consumers, obtain a greater knowledge of their requirements and worries, and customize your sales strategy to match their demands. Remember that good communication is a two-way process; therefore, it's crucial to actively listen and ask insightful questions to create trust and a relationship with your consumers.

Non-Verbal Communication in Sales

Nonverbal communication may have a big influence on sales results. Here are some strategies to utilize nonverbal communication successfully in sales:

1. **Body language:** Your body language may indicate confidence and credibility. Stand straight, keep eye contact, and avoid fidgeting or slouching.

2. **Facial expressions:** Your facial expressions may indicate a variety of emotions, such as joy, empathy, and worry. Use proper facial expressions to communicate your message successfully.

3. **Gestures:** Gestures may help you stress crucial ideas and add visual appeal to your presentation. Use motions carefully to prevent confusing your audience.

4. **Tone of speech:** Your tone of voice may indicate your attitude and feelings. Use a tone of voice suitable for the context and expresses confidence and passion.

5. **Dress:** Your dress may indicate professionalism and trustworthiness. Dress properly for the setting and ensure your clothes are clean, tidy, and professional.

6. **Personal space:** Your personal space may impact the comfort and trust your consumer feels. Respect personal space and avoid standing too near or violating personal space.

7. **Mirroring:** Mirroring the nonverbal signals of your consumer may assist in developing rapport and establishing a relationship. Match their tone,

tempo, and body language to make them feel more comfortable.

Applying these nonverbal communication skills successfully may create trust and rapport with your consumers and enhance your sales results. Remember that nonverbal communication is a strong weapon; therefore, it's crucial to utilize it wisely and correctly to deliver your message successfully.

CHAPTER EIGHT

Closing Deals and Winning Business

Closing deals and earning business is the ultimate aim of sales. Here are some tactics for completing sales and getting business:

1. **Build connections:** Building ties with your consumers is crucial to completing transactions and earning business. Establish trust and rapport with your consumers by listening intently, displaying empathy, and giving value.

2. **Understand their needs:** Understanding clients' wants is key to completing agreements. Ask open-ended questions to unearth their

trouble spots and suggest solutions matching their requirements.

3. Provide solutions that answer your clients' wants and worries. Highlight the advantages of your goods or services and explain how they may assist in solving their difficulties.

4. **Overcome objections:** Be prepared to answer objections and issues that may occur throughout the sales process. Respond to criticisms with empathy and propose solutions that solve their concerns.

5. **Create urgency:** Create a feeling of urgency by emphasizing the penalties of inactivity or the rewards of taking action immediately. Use limited-time discounts or other incentives to urge your clients to act swiftly.

6. **Close the deal:** When appropriate, ask for the sale. Use a concluding remark or question encouraging your customer to act, such as "Would you like to proceed with the purchase?" or "When would you like to schedule the service?"

7. Follow up with your consumers after the transaction to guarantee their pleasure and develop a long-term connection. Ask for feedback and utilize it to better your sales strategy in the future.

By implementing these tactics, you may close sales and win business successfully. Remember that great sales are founded on trust, empathy, and offering value to your consumers. Focus on creating great connections and understanding your client's requirements, and you will be well on your way to completing more sales and gaining more business.

Effective Closing Techniques

Effective closing strategies will allow you to seal the deal and conclude a transaction effectively. Here are some tactics that you may utilize to close more deals:

The assumptive close:

The assumptive close is a sales closing approach where the salesperson thinks the customer has already decided to acquire the product or service and offers a closing question that reflects this assumption. The assumptive closure aims to urge the consumer to make a choice without feeling rushed or pushed.

Here are some instances of assumptive closing statements:

1. "Great, we can plan the delivery for next Tuesday. Is that convenient for you?"

2. "Since you are interested in our product, would you prefer the red or the blue model?"

3. "Let's get your account set up immediately, so you can start utilizing our service right away. Shall we proceed?"

By presuming that the consumer is ready to make the purchase, the salesperson may avoid giving the buyer time to pause or second-guess their choice. The assumptive close may be a successful tactic for salespeople who have connected with the client and are certain that the consumer is interested in their product or service.

However, it's vital to utilize the assumptive closure effectively and not be overly forceful or aggressive. If the consumer is not ready to make a choice, the salesperson should accept their decision and continue to create a connection with them. The assumptive close should only be utilized when the salesperson has developed trust and rapport with the consumer and feels that the customer is ready to make a choice.

The alternate close:

The alternative close is a sales closing approach where the salesperson provides the consumer with two alternatives, both leading to a sale. The alternate closure aims to make the consumer feel powerful and in control of their choice while still directing them towards completing a purchase.

Here are some instances of alternative closing statements:

1. "Would you prefer to pay in full today, or would you prefer to finance the purchase over 6 months?"

2. "Which package option works best for you, the standard or premium package?"

3. "Would you like to proceed with the purchase today, or would you like to schedule a follow-up call to answer any questions you may have?"

By presenting the consumer with two alternatives, the salesperson may steer the customer towards deciding while enabling them to feel in charge. This strategy may be particularly helpful when the consumer is still deciding about the product or service to buy or worries about purchasing.

It's vital to utilize the alternative close wisely and not be overly pushy or aggressive. If the client requires more time to make a choice, the salesperson should respect their decision and offer to follow up later. The alternative close should only be utilized when the salesperson has developed trust and rapport with the consumer and feels that the customer is interested in purchasing.

The summary close:

The summary close is a sales closing approach where the salesperson highlights the advantages of their product or service and asks the client if they are ready to purchase. The purpose of the summary closure is to remind consumers of the value they will get from the product or service and to urge them to choose.

Here are some instances of summary closing statements:

1. "Based on what we have talked about, it seems like our product satisfies your requirements. Are you ready to make the transaction today?"

2. "So, our service will save you time and money while delivering exceptional customer care. Can we continue with the purchase now?"

3. "Just to summarize, our product includes features A, B, and C, which will tremendously help your organization. Is there anything more you need before making a choice to buy?"

By outlining the advantages of the product or service, the salesperson may remind the consumer of the value they will gain from their purchase. This may be particularly helpful when the consumer is interested in the goods but may be reluctant to choose.

It's vital to utilize the summary closely and not be overly pushy or aggressive. If the customer requires more information or time to make a choice, the salesperson should respect their decision and offer to answer any more questions they may have. The summary close should only be used when the salesperson has developed trust and rapport with the consumer and feels the customer is interested in purchasing.

The urgency close:

The urgency close is a sales closing method where the salesperson generates a feeling of urgency surrounding the transaction by stressing time-sensitive elements that may affect the customer's choice. The urgency closure aims to persuade consumers to choose immediately before they lose the chance to take advantage of the offer.

Here are some instances of urgent close statements:

1. "Our unique deal is only available for the next 24 hours. Can I assist you finish the order before it expires?"

2. "We only have a limited quantity of this product remaining in stock. Would you want to reserve your purchase before it sells out?"

3. "Our existing price is likely to rise next week. If you order now, you may take advantage of the present rate before it goes up."

By stressing time-sensitive elements, the salesperson may create a feeling of urgency surrounding the transaction and drive the buyer to make a choice soon. This strategy may be particularly helpful when the buyer is interested in the goods but may be reluctant to choose.

It's vital to utilize the urgency close wisely and not be overly pushy or aggressive. If the customer requires more information or time to make a choice, the salesperson should respect their decision and offer to answer any more questions they may have. The urgency should only be utilized when there is a true feeling of urgency and the salesman has developed a degree of trust and relationship with the consumer.

The objection close:

The objection close is a sales closing approach where the salesperson addresses any objections or worries the customer may have and gives a solution or reaction to overcome those objections. The purpose of the objection is to ease any questions or hesitations the consumer may have and urge them to choose.

Here are some instances of consolidated objection statements:

1. "I understand your anxiety about the pricing. Let me show you how our product will save you money in the long term."

2. "I know that you have some doubts regarding our service. Can you tell me more about your problems so I can address them directly?"

3. "I realize that you may be hesitant about our goods. Would you want to check it out for a trial period to see how it works for you?"

By addressing concerns and presenting solutions, the salesperson may create trust with the client and show dedication to solving the customer's requirements. This strategy may be particularly helpful when consumers have specific worries or objections that delay their choice.

It's vital to utilize the objection closely and not be overly aggressive or disrespectful of the customer's worries. The salesperson should listen intently and politely to the customer's arguments and answer with empathy and understanding. The objection should only be utilized when the salesperson has developed trust and rapport with the client and feels the consumer is interested in purchasing.

The trial close:

The trial close is a sales closing approach where the salesperson asks for feedback or a minimal commitment from the client to test their degree of interest in the product or service. The trial close aims to test the waters and determine whether the consumer is ready to go through with the purchase.

Here are some instances of trial closing statements:

1. "How does our product sound so far? Is there anything that you really enjoy or hate about it?"

2. "If we can address your concerns, would you be interested in moving forward with the purchase?"

3. "Based on what we have discussed, it appears like our service would be a good match for your requirements. Would you want to learn more about how it works?"

By asking for feedback or a little commitment, the salesperson may analyze the customer's degree of interest in the product or service and gauge their preparedness to purchase. This strategy may be particularly useful when the buyer is still contemplating and may need more time to be ready to commit to a complete purchase.

It's vital to utilize the trial close wisely and not be overly pushy or aggressive. The salesperson should listen intently and politely to the customer's reaction and reply with empathy and understanding. The trial close should only be utilized when the salesperson has developed trust and rapport with the consumer and feels the client is interested in learning more about the product or service.

Handling Negotiations

Handling negotiations is a vital ability for salespcople. Negotiations entail negotiating the terms and conditions of a transaction with a client or prospect. Here are some ways to conduct negotiations:

1. **Prepare:** Before the negotiation, analyze the customer's requirements

and objectives, and develop a list of likely objections and answers. Know your bottom line and what you are prepared to bargain on.

2. **Listen actively:** Listen to the customer's requirements and concerns during negotiations. Use open-ended inquiries to urge the consumer to offer additional information about their problem.

3. **Communicate value:** During negotiations, stress the value of your product or service and how it satisfies the customer's demands. Use case studies, testimonials, and other proof to support your assertions.

4. **investigate alternatives:** If the consumer is concerned about the conditions you have provided, investigate alternate options that may

better satisfy their requirements. Be innovative and adaptable in your approach.

5. **Stay professional:** Maintain a professional and courteous manner throughout discussions, especially if the consumer gets emotional or hostile. Avoid making personal attacks or becoming defensive.

6. **Know when to walk away:** If the negotiation is not going or the client is making unreasonable demands, it may be essential to walk away from the contract. However, always do so politely and leave the door open for future business.

Negotiating is a collaborative process, and both sides should feel they have achieved a mutually advantageous arrangement. By listening intently, expressing value, and investigating alternate alternatives, you may conduct negotiations successfully and clinch more agreements.

Securing Customer Commitment

Securing client commitment is a key phase in the sales process. It entails convincing the buyer to agree to continue with the purchase and commit to a specified activity. Here are some ways to ensure consumer commitment:

1. **Establish trust:** Building trust with the consumer is vital to ensuring their commitment. Listen attentively to their wants and concerns, and be straightforward and honest.

2. **Communicate value:** Highlight the unique value proposition of your product or service and illustrate how it fulfills the customer's particular

demands. Use case studies, testimonials, and other proof to support your assertions.

3. **Set clear expectations:** Clearly describe the terms of the agreement, including cost, delivery, and any other relevant factors. Ensure the consumer knows what they are consenting to and what they may anticipate from you.

4. **Overcome objections:** Address any worries or objections the consumer may have and propose methods to overcome them. Use strategies like the objection close and trial close to measuring their interest and commitment.

5. **Create urgency:** Encourage the consumer to act swiftly by establishing a feeling of urgency. Highlight any time-sensitive promos or offers and

underline the advantages of choosing sooner rather than later.

6. **Follow up:** Once the client has committed to the purchase, follow up swiftly to confirm the specifics and give any further information or help they may need.

Remember, gaining consumer commitment is about creating trust, presenting value, and overcoming concerns. Adopting these tactics may enhance your chances of completing more business and developing long-term connections with your consumers.

CHAPTER NINE

Managing and Nurturing Customer Relationships

Managing and developing client connections is vital for any organization that wishes to retain long-term success. Here are some ideas to assist you in properly maintaining and developing your client relationships:

Provide great client service:

Providing outstanding customer service is vital to creating good connections with customers. Here are some guidelines to help you give great customer service:

1. **Be available:** Ensure your consumers can readily contact you when needed. Provide several means of contact,

such as phone, email, chat, and social media.

2. **Respond promptly:** Respond to consumer enquiries or complaints as swiftly as feasible. Even if you don't have an instant answer, let them know that you're working on it and offer a date for when they may anticipate a resolution.

3. **Be nice:** Always be pleasant and courteous while talking with consumers. Use supportive words, listen intently to their problems, and sympathize with their circumstances.

4. **Go above and beyond:** Whenever feasible, surpass your customer's expectations. Provide additional support, give individual solutions, and ensure they feel appreciated.

5. **Solve issues fast:** If a consumer has a problem, work rapidly to remedy it. Be proactive in identifying solutions and keep the consumer updated throughout the process.

6. **Follow up:** Follow up with clients once an issue has been fixed to verify that they are happy with the solution. This indicates that you care about their experience and are devoted to their fulfillment.

7. **Train your staff:** Ensure your whole team is taught best practices on customer service. This covers communication skills, problem-solving, and how to manage unpleasant circumstances.

You may establish trust and loyalty with your consumers by offering outstanding customer service, leading to more business and favorable word-of-mouth referrals.

Build a personal connection

Building a personal connection with your consumers is a strong method to develop a long-lasting relationship. Here are some ways to help you develop a personal relationship with your customers:

1. **Show real interest:** Genuine interest in your consumers by inquiring about their requirements, preferences, and hobbies. Take the time to listen intently to their comments and use this knowledge to personalize your interactions with them.

2. **Be authentic:** Be yourself while talking with consumers. Don't pretend to be someone you're not, or use scripted replies. This will help you develop trust and credibility with your consumers.

3. **Use personalization:** Use client data to customize your conversations with them. This might involve utilizing their name in communications, making customized product suggestions, and delivering personalized notes on significant occasions.

4. **Share your narrative:** Share your personal story with your consumers. This may help people understand your beliefs and motives and build a stronger connection with your brand.

5. **Share your expertise:** Share your knowledge and experience with your customers. Offer insights, guidance, and recommendations that are relevant to their requirements.

6. **Use comedy:** Use humor in your dealings with consumers. This may help you create a more calm and

pleasurable encounter and can also assist in breaking the ice and developing rapport.

7. **Be responsive:** Respond swiftly to client requests and concerns. This indicates that you appreciate their time and are devoted to their fulfillment.

Developing a personal relationship with your clients may generate trust and loyalty, leading to repeat business and favorable word-of-mouth referrals.

Offer incentives

Offering incentives is an efficient strategy to drive clients to take action and establish loyalty. Here are some suggestions for rewards you might provide to your customers:

1. **Discounts:** provide consumers with a discount on their next purchase or if they recommend a friend to your firm.

2. **Free trials:** Offer your product or service a free trial to new clients. This enables people to test it out before committing to a purchase.

3. **Rewards programs:** Offer a rewards program that compensates clients for making recurring purchases. This may be in the form of points that can be exchanged for discounts or free products.

4. **Giveaways:** Hold giveaways or competitions that allow consumers to win a reward. This may be a fun and engaging method to develop an interest in your business.

5. **unique offerings:** Offer special deals or promotions to clients who have

been with you for a long time. This might make them feel respected and appreciated.

6. **Upgrades:** Offer clients an upgrade to a premium version of your product or service. This might be a terrific method to urge them to enhance their purchase and establish loyalty.

7. **Personalized incentives:** Offer rewards targeted to the specific consumer. This may provide special discounts for goods customers have bought or tailored suggestions for new products or services.

By delivering incentives, you drive consumers to take action and establish loyalty. Ensure that the incentives you give are relevant and helpful to your consumers and that they connect with your overall company objectives.

Use technology to remain connected

Technology may be a tremendous tool for remaining connected with clients. Here are some ways you may utilize technology to remain connected:

1. **Social media:** Use social media sites like Facebook, Twitter, and Instagram to communicate with your consumers. This might involve posting news and updates about your brand, replying to client queries and comments, and giving exceptional deals.

2. **Email marketing:** Use email marketing to maintain contact with your consumers and keep them updated about your goods, services, and promotions. Customize your

emails and segment your list depending on client interests and preferences.

3. **Customer relationship management (CRM) software:** Use a CRM system to monitor customer interactions and manage customer data. This may help you customize your client interactions and enhance the customer experience.

4. **Live chat:** Offer live chat help on your website to give clients real-time assistance. This may help you handle problems swiftly and boost client satisfaction.

5. **Mobile apps:** Develop a mobile app that enables clients to access your goods and services conveniently. This may help you keep connected with consumers even while they are on the go.

6. **Video conferencing:** Use video conferencing solutions like Zoom or Skype to engage with consumers more personally. This might be particularly advantageous for distant or virtual organizations.

By leveraging technology to keep connected with your consumers, you can enhance the customer experience and develop better connections. Select the correct tools and platforms depending on your clients' tastes and demands.

Collect and utilize consumer data

Collecting and utilizing customer data may help you better understand your consumers and offer them more tailored experiences. Here are some ways you may acquire and utilize consumer data:

1. **Customer surveys:** Use customer surveys to get feedback on your goods, services, and overall customer experience. This might help you find areas for development and better understand your client's requirements and preferences.

2. **Website analytics:** Use website analytics tools to monitor consumer activity on your website. This may help you understand which sites and goods are most popular and locations where consumers may need help.

3. **Social media analytics:** Use social media analytics tools to measure client participation on your social media platforms. This helps you identify which material forms are most popular, as well as consumer emotion towards your business.

4. **Customer relationship management (CRM) software:** Use a CRM system to monitor customer interactions and manage customer data. This may help you customize your client interactions and enhance the customer experience.

5. **Purchase history:** Use consumer purchase history to provide customized product suggestions and targeted discounts. This may help you enhance consumer loyalty and encourage repeat business.

6. **Demographic data:** Use demographic data to understand your consumer base better and customize your marketing activities appropriately. This may include criteria like age, gender, geography, and economic level.

Gathering and leveraging consumer data can create more tailored experiences and enhance the overall customer experience. Ensure you follow the best data privacy and security practices and be honest with consumers about how their data will be used.

Reward loyalty

Rewarding loyalty is an excellent strategy for creating long-term client connections. Here are some ways you may thank loyal customers:

1. **Loyalty programs:** Offer a loyalty program that rewards consumers for recurring purchases. This may be in the form of points that can be exchanged for discounts or free products.

2. **unique promotions**: Offer unique promotions and discounts to loyal clients. This might make customers feel valued and appreciated and encourage them to continue doing business with you.

3. **customized offers:** Offer customized offers to loyal consumers based on their purchasing history and preferences. This might offer discounts on goods they have already bought or tailored suggestions for new products or services.

4. **Exclusive access:** Offer exclusive access to new items or services to loyal consumers before making them accessible to the broader public. This may make customers feel unique and valued and can develop enthusiasm around your business.

5. **VIP events:** Host VIP events or experiences for loyal consumers. This may include things like exclusive shopping events, exclusive product demonstrations, or meet & greets with corporate officials.

By rewarding loyalty, you may develop deeper connections with your consumers and encourage them to continue doing business with you. Choose appropriate and useful consumer incentives that connect with your overall company objectives.

Continuously improve

Continuous improvement is a critical part of developing long-term client connections. Here are some ways you may continually improve to serve your customers better:

1. **Customer input:** Collect feedback from your customers regularly. This might include surveys, reviews, and direct feedback. Use this input to find areas for improvement and make required modifications.

2. **Employee training:** Give your workers continual training and development opportunities to ensure they are prepared with the knowledge and abilities to give great customer care.

3. **Process improvement:** Continuously analyze your company processes to discover opportunities for improvement. This might involve simplifying procedures to make them more efficient or establishing new processes to serve your consumers better.

4. **Innovation:** Stay up-to-date with the newest technology and trends in your sector to guarantee you give your consumers the most inventive and valued goods and services.

5. **Metrics tracking:** Set metrics to monitor and assess your success in critical areas, including customer happiness, client retention, and revenue growth. Use this data to discover areas for improvement and measure progress over time.

By consistently upgrading, you may create better client experiences and establish deeper connections with them over time. Make sure to engage your clients in the process and keep them aware of any modifications or enhancements you are making.

Managing Customer Feedback and Reviews

Managing client comments and reviews is vital to creating and maintaining a great reputation for your organization. Here are some strategies for handling client feedback and reviews:

1. **Monitor feedback and reviews:** Monitor feedback and frequent reviews to keep updated about what your consumers say about your goods and services. This may include social media platforms, review sites, and other online forums.

2. **Respond immediately:** Respond swiftly to consumer comments and reviews, both good and bad. This demonstrates that you respect their opinion and are dedicated to fixing difficulties.

3. **Address negative comments:** Address negative feedback in a productive and empathic way. Acknowledge the customer's problems and give a remedy or reimbursement if applicable.

4. **Use the input to improve:** Use consumer feedback to find areas for improvement in your goods, services, and overall customer experience. Make modifications and improvements based on client input to demonstrate that you are listening and devoted to delivering the greatest possible experience for your consumers.

5. **Encourage favorable reviews:** Encourage pleased customers to submit positive feedback on review sites and social media outlets. This helps counterbalance unfavorable

reviews and develop a good reputation for your firm.

6.   **Thank consumers for their input:** Thank customers for their good and negative feedback. This indicates that you respect their advice and are determined to utilize it to better your firm.

By efficiently handling customer comments and reviews, you can develop a solid reputation for your organization and enhance the customer experience. Make sure to keep involved with your consumers and utilize their comments to continue to improve.

CHAPTER TEN

Social Selling

Social selling is utilizing social media to form connections, generate trust, and sell items or services. Here are some guidelines for efficient social selling:

1. Identify your target audience: Identify and understand their wants and pain points. This will assist you in personalizing your social media material to their interests and demands.

2. create connections: Use social media to connect with future consumers. Engage with them on social media by liking, commenting, and sharing their

stuff. This helps to develop trust and credibility.

3. Provide value to your followers by giving relevant information, industry insights, and helpful advice. This helps position you as an authority in your sector and generate trust with prospective consumers.

4. Showcase your goods or services: Showcase your products or services on social media by publishing product demonstrations, customer testimonials, and other relevant information. Add calls to action to urge prospective consumers to take the next step.

5. Leverage social media advertising: Use social media advertising to reach a bigger audience and target certain demographics. This may assist in

attracting visitors to your website and improve revenue.

6. Measure and adapt: Measure the effectiveness of your social selling activities and alter your plan as required. Use analytics like engagement, click-through rates, and conversions to assess what works and needs improvement.

By efficiently utilizing social media for selling, you may form closer connections with prospective consumers, establish trust, and eventually improve sales. Make sure to give value, connect with your audience, and continually assess your performance to improve your social selling plan.

Using Social Media Platforms for Sales

Social media platforms may be excellent tools for sales since they enable companies to communicate with prospective consumers and advertise goods or services. Here are some strategies for leveraging social media platforms for sales:

1. **Choose the correct platforms:** Identify the social media channels that are most relevant to your target demographic. This may include platforms like Facebook, Instagram, LinkedIn, and Twitter.

2. **Optimize your accounts:** Make sure your social media profiles are thoroughly optimized with a professional profile image, cover photo, and bio. Include information about your firm, goods, and services.

3.   **Share relevant material:** Share relevant and beneficial stuff with your target audience. This may contain blog entries, industry news, product updates, and client testimonials.

4.   **Engage with your audience:** Engage with your audience by replying to comments and messages and sharing and commenting on their work. This helps to form connections and establish trust.

5.   **Use social media advertising:** Use social media advertising to reach a bigger audience and target certain demographics. This may be an efficient technique to market items or services and increase visitors to your website.

6.   **Monitor analytics:** Monitor analytics to monitor the efficacy of your social

media sales initiatives. Use analytics like engagement, click-through rates, and conversions to assess what works and needs improvement.

By utilizing social media platforms successfully for sales, companies can interact with prospective consumers, create connections, and eventually improve sales. Create good material, communicate with your audience, and continually assess your effectiveness to improve your social media sales plan.

Creating Compelling Social Content

Creating captivating social media content is vital for attracting the attention of your audience and increasing interaction. Here are some strategies for developing intriguing social content:

1. **Know your audience:** Understand your target audience and their interests, preferences, and requirements. This will assist you to generate content that is relevant and interesting to them.

2. **Use eye-catching pictures:** Use high-quality visuals, such as photographs, movies, and graphics, to attract the attention of your audience. Make sure your images are on-brand and aesthetically attractive.

3. **Tell a story:** Use narrative strategies to make your material more fascinating and engaging. Create a story that connects with your audience and keeps them fascinated.

4. **Use humor:** Humor can be a strong technique for engaging your audience and making your content more shareable. Use comedy in a tasteful

manner that is consistent with your brand voice and values.

5. **Be authentic:** Authenticity is crucial to developing trust with your audience. Be real and truthful in your social media posting, and avoid overly promotional or sales language.

6. Provide value to your audience by giving important information, industry insights, and helpful advice. This helps position you as an authority in your business and generate trust with your audience.

7. **Use calls-to-action:** Use calls-to-action to urge your audience to take the next step, such as visiting your website, signing up for your newsletter, or purchasing.

By developing captivating social media content, companies can attract their audience's attention, increase interaction, and eventually accomplish their marketing goals. Make sure to know your audience, utilize eye-catching pictures, tell a narrative, be real, give value, and use calls-to-action to make your social media material more successful.

CHAPTER ELEVEN

Business Opportunities for You

Digital Marketing

Digital marketing uses digital media for advertising goods or services and engaging consumers. It comprises a variety of approaches and strategies that exploit digital channels, such as search engines, social media platforms, email, and websites, to reach target audiences and accomplish marketing goals.

Here are some typical forms of digital marketing:

1. **Search engine optimization (SEO):** SEO entails improving your website's ranking in search engine results pages (SERPs). This incorporates tactics like keyword research, on-page optimization, and link building.

2. **Pay-per-click advertising (PPC):** includes posting advertisements on search engine results on pages or social media platforms and paying each time a person clicks on an ad. This may be an efficient approach to attract visitors to your website and create leads.

3. **Social media marketing:** Social media marketing utilizes platforms like Facebook, Twitter, Instagram, or LinkedIn to promote goods or services, engage with consumers, and develop brand recognition.

4. **information marketing:** Content marketing entails developing and sharing quality information, such as blog posts, infographics, or videos, to attract and engage a target audience.

5. **Email marketing:** Email marketing includes sending promotional emails or newsletters to a list of subscribers to advertise items or services, establish connections, and drive sales.

6. **Influencer marketing:** Influencer marketing entails collaborating with influencers or persons with big social media followings to promote goods or services to their audiences.

Digital marketing provides a multitude of advantages, including enhanced brand exposure, enhanced search engine presence, increased website traffic, and improved client interaction. By adopting various digital marketing tactics, firms may reach their target audience successfully and accomplish their marketing goals.

E-commerce

E-commerce, short for electronic commerce, refers to the purchasing and selling of products and services online via digital channels such as websites, mobile applications, and social media platforms. E-commerce has risen significantly over the last two decades and is a key driver of worldwide retail sales.

Here are some major components of e-commerce:

1. **Online storefront:** An online storefront is the digital version of a

physical shop. It is the website or platform where clients may explore and buy items or services.

2. **Payment processing:** Payment processing refers to the technology and systems used to process and collect payments from clients securely. This covers credit cards, digital wallets, and other payment methods.

3. **Logistics and fulfillment:** Logistics and fulfillment are related to the procedures involved in delivering things from the seller to the client, including shipping, tracking, and inventory management.

4. **Customer service:** Customer service is a vital component of e-commerce since consumers may have queries or concerns linked to their transactions. E-commerce enterprises must be responsive and deliver exceptional

customer service to develop customer trust and loyalty.

5. **Marketing and advertising:** E-commerce enterprises must properly market their goods or services to attract consumers and increase sales. This may entail leveraging various digital marketing channels such as search engine optimization, paid advertising, social media, and email marketing.

E-commerce provides several advantages to organizations, including broader reach, cheaper administrative expenses, and better flexibility. However, it also brings certain problems, including security issues, logistical complications, and extreme competitiveness. To compete in a fast-shifting digital world, successful e-commerce firms must be adaptable, inventive, and customer-focused.

Affiliate marketing

Affiliate marketing is a performance-based marketing technique where an advertiser (or merchant) pays a commission to an affiliate for promoting their goods or services and generating traffic or purchases to their website. An affiliate is generally a third-party person or organization that advertises the items or services on its website or social media platforms.

Here are the essential components of affiliate marketing:

1. **Merchant:** The merchant is the company that sells items or services for sale and is aiming to boost its online visibility and sales.

2. **Affiliate:** An affiliate is a person or organization who promotes the merchant's goods or services on their website or social media platforms.

3. **Affiliate network:** An affiliate network operates as an intermediary between the merchant and the affiliate. The network offers a platform for monitoring sales and commissions and administering payments to affiliates.

4. **Commission:** The commission is the reward that the affiliate gets from the merchant for marketing their goods or services and creating sales or traffic.

5. **monitoring:** Affiliate marketing depends significantly on monitoring to assess the performance of programs effectively. This involves measuring clicks, impressions, conversions, and other crucial performance indicators.

Affiliate marketing may be an efficient strategy for companies to enhance their online presence and boost sales, enabling them to tap into the reach and influence of affiliates to advertise their goods or services. However, it also takes rigorous planning and execution to guarantee that the program is lucrative and sustainable over the long run. Successful affiliate marketing programs involve strong connections between merchants and affiliates and reliable monitoring, reporting, and payment systems.

Freelancing

Freelancing is a work arrangement where a self-employed person delivers their skills to customers on a project-by-project basis rather than being hired by a corporation full-time or part-time. Freelancers are commonly employed to handle specialized activities, such as writing, graphic design, programming, or marketing.

Here are the fundamental components of freelancing:

1. **Services offered:** Freelancers provide several services to customers, such as writing, editing, design, development, marketing, and consulting.

2. **customers:** Freelancers work for customers requiring certain jobs or projects. Clients may be people or corporations.

3. **Rates and payment:** Freelancers determine their rates and are responsible for invoicing customers and collecting money for their services.

4. **Work arrangements:** Freelancers may work from home or a distant location and work on many projects simultaneously for various customers.

5. **Portfolio:** A freelancer's portfolio is a collection of their work demonstrating their talents and abilities to prospective customers.

Freelancing may provide several advantages, such as flexibility, autonomy, and the chance to work on various projects for various customers. However, it may also be tough since freelancers are responsible for finding their customers, managing their workload, and handling administrative chores such as billing and taxes.

Successful freelancers must be self-motivated, organized, and competent at managing their time and resources. They must also communicate effectively with customers, create realistic objectives and deadlines, and provide high-quality work on time and within budget.

Real estate

Real estate refers to the purchasing, selling, renting, and managing of properties, including land, buildings, and residences. Real estate is a tough market that includes various participants, including agents, brokers, developers, investors, and property managers.

Here are the essential components of real estate:

1. **Properties:** Real estate is all about properties, including land, buildings, and residences. These might be residential, commercial, or industrial.

2. **Real estate agents and brokers:** Real estate agents and brokers are registered professionals who assist customers in purchasing, selling, and renting properties. They get a commission on each transaction.

3. **Developers:** Developers are responsible for establishing new properties, including land development and building projects.

4. **Investors:** Real estate investors acquire properties intending to generate a return on their investment via rental income or an increase in property value.

5. **Property managers:** Property managers handle the day-to-day operations of rental properties, including leasing, maintenance, and tenant relations.

Real estate may be a booming sector, but it also takes a large commitment of time and money. Successful real estate professionals must have good communication and negotiating skills and a profound awareness of market trends and property prices. They must also manage their time well and maintain strong relationships with customers, renters, and other stakeholders.

CHAPTER TWELVE

Conclusion

In conclusion, current selling strategies have developed greatly in recent years due to technological improvements and client behavior changes. With the development of social media, digital marketing, and e-commerce, sales professionals can access new tools and channels for reaching and connecting with clients.

To thrive in contemporary selling, sales professionals must be versatile and open to adopting new tactics and technology. They need to have great communication and relationship-building abilities and a comprehensive awareness of their target clients' wants and preferences. By utilizing data and analytics to tailor their approach, using social media and other digital platforms to contact consumers, and consistently upgrading their skills and approaches, sales professionals may remain ahead of the curve and succeed in today's competitive industry.

www.ingramcontent.com/pod-product-compliance
Lightning Source LLC
Chambersburg PA
CBHW070540220526
45467CB00003B/1003